"Frail children of dust...."

From "O Worship the King," No. 26 in
   The Hymnbook Published by
   The Presbyterian Church in the United States

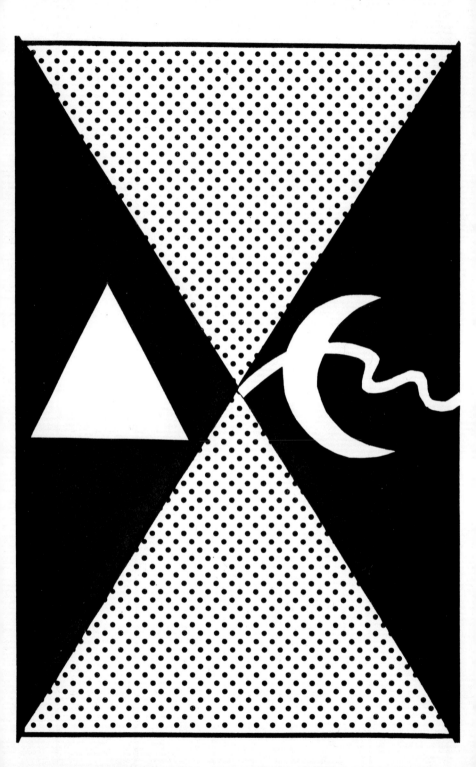

CHILDREN OF DUST
Portraits & Preludes

Poems by
Elisabeth Stevens

Volume XII

THE NEW POETS SERIES, INC.
Baltimore, Maryland 1985

Cover and illustrations designed by the author.

Editor/Publisher:
Clarinda Harriss Lott

This volume was partially funded by grants from the Maryland State Arts
Council and MAC/AC (The Mayor's Advisory Council on Art & Culture).

ISBN Number: 0-932616-15-1
Library of Congress Number: 85-060055

Certain poems in this collection have appeared in the following publications:
*Baltimore Scene, Best Articles & Stories, City Paper, Confrontation, Epos,
Harbor Lights, Quicksilver, Portland Review, Riverside Poetry, Soundings, Wind.*

In Memory Of My Mother

Table of Contents

II. Preludes

I

Portraits

Emily, straight as a bed post
Was wont to talk of love
Softly
Alone on the front porch
Amidst white iron arm chairs
And well trained ivy leaves.

"The love that I loved was a beautiful love
In the day of the green locust and the wild hibiscus,
Yet I could not love the mirror
For it showed, maliciously,
A strange woman in a brown dress,
A vaguely despicable creature
A person I would not have cared to meet
Suddenly, at a sharp turning.
I could not love that mirror,
And I could not love my love
Properly
As the sun loves the grass —
Warmly....

The worm suns himself on the sidewalk,
The six o'clock whistle blows,
Emily coughs and goes in for dinner.

"You, Anne,
Remind me of that portrait of
Myself as I was then, your pale
Pale skin and hair that's combed straight down
To dark inquisitive brows —
Charming!"

The child
Regards the crimson hat above
The lady's dead red curls and then
The face on which the make-up clings
Like mouldy cheese near big lolly-
Pop eyes.

Anne knows
The lady lies, this often is
The way of grownups teasing her.
And yet she sees the lady could
Quick catch kiss her to coo a cruel
Byebye.

The tall ancestral figures
Form a disapproving circle,
Looking down, laughing,
Shaking their heads.

These constraining statues,
Narrow rods of dead coldness,
Are impossible to escape
Because they stand too close together.

Caught in the center,
A prisoner in their circle,
Sink to your knees, cover your face,
Beg.

> "To know how to free oneself is nothing: the arduous
> thing is to know what to do with one's freedom."
> Andre Gide *The Immoralist*

Freedom is a series of white doors
Laid open between echo empty halls.
Rebels float through successive thresholds
With never the scuff of a footstep.
Admiring cold pink mirror floors.

And floating they long for the
Cluttered, curtained, hearth-warm room,
To lie, heavy, curled on the
Familiar round rug and dream
Of the dance without moving.

Floaters — indefinite hordes in the halls —
You are insubstantial and beautiful
As milkweed, brushing by, embracing air,
Gliding like vapors — bumping and sliding —
Magnificent, pointless, green silk balloons!

Black is sharp
A violent color
For a woman
Whose hands are always clenched
Against her lap,
Fingers entwined, pinioned
So they cannot pick, pinch, stab.

Chatter, bitter clatter
Her mouth is a castanet,
Like the newly blind,
She shrills strangled anger —
Beats against the panes —
Demanding morning.

Through the shiny licorice phone
I felt
Her lean yellow pencil fingers
Catching in my hair
And pulling,

And her fast
Neverwillstop
Voice

Drawing me through the receiver
Into the long black rubber wire
Of the phone.

Some women

Some women
Have minds wound up like clocks.
Their thoughts
Are ants swarming on fallen sugar.

Like lead bags
Of feathers,
They weigh,
They smother.

Yet they are
Fragile.
They must be
Smiled at

So that their
Babyblue eyes
Will not brim with
Beads of mercury.

Things must be
Pointed out to them,
And for as long as possible,
They will pretend not to understand.

They always look the other way.
They will not see us
Bending under their weight,
Breaking.

Librarian

Faded virgin
Pressed thin as pages,
She flounces in flowered garments,
Curls, and blue glass earrings.
She is pleased to tell you,
After you have completed all her forms
In the one proper way,
"This book can't circulate, you know,
Sign this last card, and you may read it here."

Miss Leclerc

From eyes like dingy pool of unshed years.
She now surveys the keys
Of her typewriter,
All others having been lost or dropped
When the doors began to shut,
Softly as shadows
Slowly as her fingers now touch
These forty shining noiseless easytouch keys
To reproduce
Words.

Men

Breakers of hymens
And of the best Venetian glass vase
That always stood at the end of the mantel,
They scuff rugs

And stretch wombs.
Muddy and hairy,
Rushing in too quickly
At the wrong time,

They are
Loud confusers of order —
Spattering blood
On white stones in formal gardens.

A man who wipes his mouth twice

A man
Who wipes his mouth twice
And piles potato skins neatly
At the edge of his plate
Is a slow, limpid lover.

He takes his pleasure
Like a boy
Who strips living petals
And stamps them up the steps
In a white, ascending line.

One plays the giant.
Moving hugely on legs like steep towers,
She surveys her realm,
Striding enormously as though on stilts,
Slapping her thigh and
Laughing roughly like a young huntsman.

And yet the second,
Sitting stolid as a clean prize sow,
Dignified and gray,
Is never offended as the tall one
Stalks near her, pacing
Off an established territory.

And as the rough brown hunting words
Pause
The older fat one simpers and
Emits
From somewhere deep between her legs
The coo
Of a littlegirlgurgling laugh.

The bitterness of women is like mold
Soft
Spreading meaninglessly without direction.

A cancer
It destroys in the dark
Hidden and incurable.

Watch out for them
When they toss bouquets of fear into the air
Like flowers.

Riders

Little boys on big bicycles
Ride deserted campus paths in summer.
They are circling the chapel,
Leaning backwards,
No hands.
And now they are coasting
Down behind the elms.
Cut off, reappearing, skimming tree shadows.
They glide in and out,
Aimless as August,
Going somewhere...anywhere...nowhere....

She will not stay long anywhere.
With age she desires new rooms,
Steel kitchens and walls
Without finger prints.
She rearranges furniture
Like cups on a mantel.

At first each place is perfect —
A love, a darling, a dream.
Then quickly, it shows cracks, faults.
It betrays her.
It is no longer what she expected.
She grows rebellious, angry, righteous,
Makes secret plans at night,
And suddenly, turns away.

She has found a *new* place,
She is going to *move!*
It is a glorious adventure —
The beginning of a perfect arrangement.

Pausing
On the threshold
Of wet snow kisses,
Capriciously delightful
White floating feathers,
She lingers almost giggling,
Fingering a fur imagination —
Her soft delightful armor.

"Mother —
The snow — perhaps I won't walk —
Today."

The image is so lovely
Of her form in the doorway
She dreams whimsical tickle
Snowflakes must withdraw
In empty windwhirls
Without so much as touching
The half-delighted figure
In a doorway —
        Pausing.

The wives of old, important men
Are fluttery, gracefully wrinkled.
They wear limp, overpatterned dresses
Or expensive, frumpish suits.
Like ageing paperdolls
They are flat and brittle,
Spotted with faint brown marks.

Their husbands roar continually,
But with decreasing vigor,
"Money...Power...Fame...."
And the wives smile and nod, smile and nod.
The husbands growl, baring yellowed teeth.
And the wives listen, and say
The things they have always said.

Their heads bob with yesses,
Like china dolls'
Their wide eyes blink
Open — then shut.
Open
Then shut.

In an old square black truck
With a noisy motor,
The linen man comes
On Mondays.

Whistling, he brings
New sheets
Neatly folded
And takes away

The other ones which lie
In redolent, wrinkled mounds
In the hallways
Outside the rooms.

The sweat, the tears
The softly curling,
Displaced hairs
Will be

Washed away
Or ironed flat
After being bleached
And counted.

The places where
Our hands were
And our bodies
Touched

Will be occupied
By others
Who will make
New wrinkles

And temporary,
Almost invisibile marks
Until Monday,
When the linen man comes back

Whistling.

I. *Dr. Zavrod*

Dr. Zavrod is a gentle, sixtyish person in a grey suit.
He listens to my lung under my shoulder blade,
And through the ribs in front.
Deep breath, cough, deep breath, cough again.

When he is through, opening the white curtains around the bed,
I ask for the verdict.
Then he sits down and tells me about the tumor and how
"They do wonderful things with cobalt treatments these days."

II. *Dr. Maier*

Dr. Maier looks like Santa Claus
In spite of his black suit.
He asks many questions,
And is kind.

He puts an arm over my shoulders
And tells me I don't have a tumor
But he will have to operate
Anyway.

They are turning the woman whose spine they operated on yesterday,
    Father, Our Father.
They are turning her because she should not be too long on
    one side — for circulation.
They are turning her so the fluid will not gather in her lungs
    and start pneumonia.
They are turning her to change the sheets.

They are raising her for the bed pan
Which she needs every half hour or so,
Because the I.V. fluid, dripping from a bottle into the vein
    of her arm,
Goes right through her.

All night long they are turning Maria Puglese from Palermo,
    Father.
Kind nurses, clumsy nurses, the breezy girl from Dublin and
    the ugly one in the grey uniform who has promised to
    pray for her.
Pray for Maria Puglese
Pray.

Like a bird on a string I
Fly and come back to him
Fly and come back to him.

Alighting on his shoulder,
Nudging my way inside
His great brown jacket

Against his breast.
And there, in the darkness
Surrounded by the warm smell

Of his flesh,
I make my nest.
Softer than straw

Are his hairs that curl
Against my feathers.
Lighter than the wind,

Is his touch
Against my beak.
And so, secure,

I hesitate to
Emerge, open my wings
Hover with the eagles.

Yet I remember
As if from a different lifetime,
The way south —

The sea, the farthest islands
The highest clouds.
And so, circling his head lovingly,

I pull against the string
Lightly, persistently.
Willing to wear the collar forever

But begging him to release me —
Eager to go, sure to return,
And always afraid of

His gun.

The old woman
Who had gone the half mile trail and back
With the other vacationers, tottering along on a stick,
Fell just as we were approaching the motorboats
That would take us back.

"Don't touch me," she said
As she lay with a root
Arching her back,
But after a moment the men lifted her
And she sat up, rubbing herself.

One of her daughters, the married one,
Helped her. But the other —
The one with the cropped hair,
Little silver cross pendant and bifocals,
(She looked middle aged but was younger)

Only called her dog — a honey colored mongrel —
And turned in the other direction,
Climbing into the prow of the biggest boat
As though it had all
Happened before.

They got the old woman into the stern
And then I remembered how,
Back at the falls after we'd eaten,
She'd tried to tell me something odd
About her dead husband.

But instead
(I wanted to wade alone
In the place where the streams crossed,
And the waters eddied white)
I slipped away.

Even back there,
It was as though she wanted to fall —
Just to show she could get up again.
And in the boat — when they finally got it started —
She offered all the children soda crackers from a half-eaten pack.

Finally, half way across the lake,
She took a small green bottle of mouthwash from her pocket,
And unscrewed it,
Smiling as though it were an elixir
The rest of us didn't have.

Shadows that pass
Flowing...
Sand through a glass
Falling....

The nice lives
Of nice people
Are clean stones
Lining nameless rivers.

They are smoothed,
Ground to sand,
Causing no ripples.

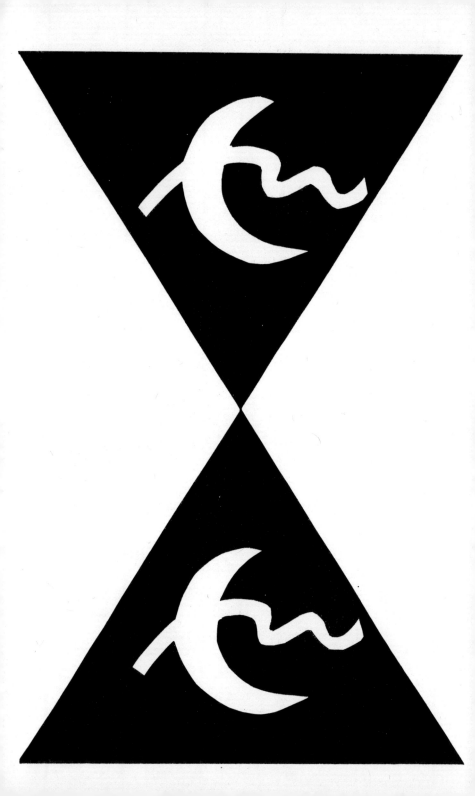

II

Preludes

Leaving all meanings behind

Leaving all meanings behind
To go quietly, drained of fear,
To an empty field by a soft brown sea
And there to be with my love
Without words and without moving:
This, in one day of a lifetime,
Is sufficient.

Children in blue

Children in blue on a perhaps green field, a
Tongue that is clenched in the jaws of the city....
Watching them we the two, eternal, hand in hand
Evoked half-slumbering by an almost spring.

What if we should ask the question? No. Why
Should we not subtract a kiss because it is too
Early? Is not retreat the beating of a wind still cold?
Yet...but come, time works, the subway is a warm cocoon.

A fine rain finishes winter

A fine rain finishes winter.
Its slanting falling
Deepens dust pink buildings
To brown.

Green and yellow umbrellas
Unfurl in doorways
Revolve
Collapse and hang limply.

Slow are
The awakenings
The soft tread beginnings
Of other lives.

Permanent Exhibit

Preparing the exhibition,
Sculptors carry their sculpture,
Dead stone weights
Almost equal to their own.
Hands, heads, torsos
Are fitted to white slabs.
Half bodies in marble
Will gather the weight of years
And at last carry easily
Their insubstantial sculptors
Long since disassembled.

A night foghorn from the river
Wet trumpets spring,
Flooding brittle air
With lumpy summer sap.

The high green fences between gardens
Mildew and bulge,
And through each hidden breach
The cats crawl
Visiting noisily in last summer's stubble.

I float out on my mattress
And throw my white nightgown
To the dark-brown-smelling river,
Hover haughty, high and lonely,
Awake in spite of cloud-cooled sheets.

Seventy Fourth and Park
The thinness of
An old woman's
Legs. The stalks of
A dead azalea.
Hairs on white linen.

Eighty Second and Fifth
Boatloads of pigeons
Nesting like marmots,
Cluttering,
Confusing.
Complicating the calm grey squares
Of the wet granite sidewalk.

Ninety Sixth and Broadway
New York was a subway color
Rusted by rains.
Pink and red umbrellas
Circled sidewalk gratings.
And then in the dampness
I recalled
Your warm white sponge petal flesh.

November recalls nothing
If not our love.
Short days, long nights
Drawn blinds, half light.
Our confused fusion —
A blanket spread by you
Against world wet,
Malaise and winter cough —
November sees destroyed.

November strips us white. Raw,
Naked, we poise, facing
Each other — the first time.
I feel your winter eyes
And hide my frozen mouth
With damp inadequate
Hands. Your discontent, like
Brown ground, drains each kiss cold.
November…grey branches break with snow….

Between midnight and the perhaps chance
Of dawn, I wander,
Crossing brown shale paths,
Turning and returning
To the same place —
A grove of poplars,
Hushed, flickering with starlight,
Pointing in all directions.

I will not hear their questions,
The thousand rustling starlight whispers,
And I will not watch the grey wind
Pirouetting in those branches. No,
I shall rush to a new tree and a new turning....
But the path is never the same one,
And the black starlight has deceived me.
I stand in frozen grass — facing the same place.

The stars have drowned in the heavens
And the moon is a cold sea green.
I crawl on the red shale pathways,
Passing trees, dry and barren, branches uplifted,
Scraping the pane of the sky.
I make no sign. I am almost there.
I have returned to the grove of poplars
Pointing in all directions.

The pattern of the ceiling with its interlacing flowers
Hangs above my feeling on a smoky yellow morning,
And between is a long glass chandelier.
There are flowers in the ceiling that were twisted by the artist

Through the long strong tendrils of a yellow brown vine.
And the blue of the flowers and the rose in the center
Is covered by the vine leaves that are growing in the ceiling.
And the vine is encompassing and forms a little border

Of the geometric vine leaves that were traced by the artist
And painted grey and rose.
As I lie beneath the ceiling I am watching for the flowers,
I will drag away the vine leaves and their interlacing tendrils.

I will pull away the pattern and its ghastly repetition
And tear down the long strong brown vine.
But the air is so yellow on a thick smoky morning
It is hard to touch the ceiling, and the vine leaves are elusive.

And from a cluster of the vines in the center of the ceiling
Hangs a long, glass, pointed, Venetian chandelier.

Mute as trees,
We watch love
Turned
Between us like an amber leaf
Whipped
Through gutters on the dust of seeds
Rasped
Away on the gravel path
Ripped
At last in the needle grass.

Then we
Rush to recrimation
Snatch
Greedily at wind
Race
To whet our axes
If only on ourselves.

Brown morning rains fall,
Closing the circle of passion.
The curtains that shrouded the cowering
Are drawn back.
A watch is wound, the clock moves to strike.
A yellow plant, set on the sill, sucks
Rusty water that is jumping methodically
Off the high, overhanging roof.

Ashtrays are emptied, pillows puffed, kisses
Considered, embraces rationalized.
The mirror reflects an empty hallway, the grey-green
Dust that gives substance to the faded upholstery
Reassumes its voiceless shape.
Flesh is inviolable, bearing no imprints.
The mind will whir and writhe
And readjust.

Heavy brown summer
Settles down
With rain.

The sky
Is a white celluloid
Sun.

Dampness
Presses the curtains
On the windows,

Tightens
About the waist
Like a yellow sash.

Each breath —
A colorless staccato flower —
Diminishes air.

Ashes in a shallow cup
Are
Shifted by waves
Of warm air.

The moon
Is not quite full
A bitten apple
Yellow as a harvest pear.

Where is he
Now that we are separated
By this sultry night
Of sullen misunderstanding?

Summer rain.
An old woman's hand at the window wipes the ledge with
    a small sponge.
The enduring Hand Laundryman removes the water from the
    domino block of his threshold with a red straw broom.
A hard rain.
The widening water comes around the corner in the gutter
    carrying castaways of crumpled white paper.
A curved blue woman sews before a closed window and from
    behind her chair a man in a white undershirt stands
    Staring down the rain.
There is a squashed, soggy silence and a stoppage of movement
And the water comes in streams from the red block rear of
    the parked newspaper truck.
The button-bulging gentleman without umbrella withdraws
    impatiently beneath an insufficient triangular cornice
    and damply reflects,
Rain is a time between....

After it stops,
Stampled against the black washed mirror of the street are
    unexplainable sodden pieces of yellow, blue and pink
    confetti.
An enormous van mounts to the corner cradling only
    a broken brown sofa emitting springs and an
    abandoned stove stiffly displaying legs like
    white stalks.
And a girl comes out from a doorway swinging a furled red
    umbrella by its cane curved handle in a capricious circle
    around her hand.

When I've paid all my dues
To names, places, must and ought,

I'm going to make
A blue gardenia

Out of long sheets of tissue paper
And the thinnest possible wire.

And when the whole thing is finished,
I'll raise it above my head like a soft umbrella,

Then light it
So ashes will come down like rain

On my hair, my shoulders, my hands,
And then drift

To the sea behind me
An offering for an outgoing tide.

That almost-spring day
When we took the old train
Early in the morning,
There was water in the woods.

Dark pools
Lying between winter trees
Oozing into the meadows,
Rising to white clapboard houses.

We were going to the circus,
You and I
Mother and child,
Our long-awaited day together.

And it was all there ahead of us
Promises, clowns,
Summer, harvest,
Like the water — rising.

I must go to the church now.
Someone is waiting at the facade,
Between the trees. I remain here
Among clean white slabs —
The cool tombs, the shade, the flies.

But glaring from the tomb fronts
Are their eyes, the black cemetery eyes.
The photographs in medallion
Of Papa and the professor and
The baby banked with roses.

And all their eyes are open;
They follow wide down the pathways;
And from behind the cypresses, watch.
They surround me
In carefully prepared boxes.

There are more dead than living.
I have no box.
But someone is waiting at
The green-red-gold
Patterned church front.

I must go out.
They say.

A poem comes
Like a small boat
Approaching the shore.

Just after sundown,
Gliding over calm water,
First you see the shadow.

Then, as the dark shape approaches,
There is definition —
A prow, a mast,

The slap of waves against the hull,
A single light.
The arrival is quiet —

Only the scraping of the keel
Furrowing the sand,
Then footsteps.

Dark figures disembark,
Pattern the tide line,
Then scatter.

Soon there is nothing but
The moonlight, the sand,
And the quiet repetition of the waves.

In the private library
Under concealing carved oak tables,
Feet shuffle.

There are accidental encounters,
Hidden bumpings,
Apologies and withdrawals.

Eyes meet
Above green glass lamp shades —
And veer away.

A thumb explores an ear lobe,
A finger peruses the inner edge
Of a silent lip.

Each reader is bound by a Morocco volume,
And the books are shelved by subjects.
War, peace, life, art are

Alphabetized and numbered
In arched shelves between
Casements curtained with brown velvet.

There is a long golden hair on this table
Lying between us like a message.
I do not know you,

I will not know you.
Yet why are your feet continually shuffling?
And what are you doing

With the hand that is
Beneath the table
Where I cannot see?

Through the night crack
In the winter window,
A spume of fog
Spirals toward the bed.

It expands
Through the coils of the springs,
Dampens the mattress,
Seeps between the sheets.

Soon,
We are lying on a white sea,
Merging like clouds
As it rises around us.

I am not afraid,
I am in your arms.
Together we float,
As the fog tide rises.

How can it be?
We are gliding through the window,
Circling leftover snow piles
And the icy tips of trees.

Where are we going?
Down the quiet street,
Beyond the lamplight,
To the forest, the hills, the sea.

Wherever the fog carries us,
We will be there together,
Our bodies relaxed, transparent,
White as shades, whiter than the mist.

There is a lassitude,
A lack of definition.
We are merging into the fog
That carries us.

Part of it.
Part of each other.
Part of others forever gone.

What has happened?
Why is everything so quiet?

Is there no one laughing in
The next room, the next house, the next life?

Why are all the voices stilled?
Nothing. No one moving.

My cheek is cold.
My skin feels like glass.

Will I always be holding this pencil.
Writing on this paper?

Has time stopped?
Will I, the survivor,

Always be lying
Waiting for you in this bed?

Perhaps
A year of so from now,
We will all be refugees
In a wooden cart

Fleeing down a rutted road
With the fire sky behind us
And the conditions ahead
Umber, scumbled, uncertain.

I will be clutching something
Inconsequential —
A spoon, a stalk of corn
A broken shoe lace —

Nothing of value.
All that — consumed.
And because of the unaccustomed
Lightness, I giggle,

Never screaming until
They try to make me unloose
The fingers of your
Grey, stiffening hand.

I have galloped through plains
And over mountains.
Now I am settled
In this green and peaceful valley.

After battles and cities,
A tent of hides,
A well-tended hearth,
A familiar stream.

And who
From this land of corn and honey
Would want to push on
To the last, cold sea?

Let the horses graze.
Stay, watch the sunsets.
Suck the bones from the pot.
Even they — are sweet.

The bodies I have lain by,
The blazing funeral pyres,
All lie behind me —
Like the wake of a wave.

I have lost gold bracelets in the sand,
Buried lovers,
Broken saddles,
Shattered cups on distant stones.

Why strike the tents?
Except — the horses are neighing,
The sun is coming again from the south,
The morning smells...green.

Rest, wait. Yet warming myself,
I know the coals will darken.
I will kick them aside.
I will saddle the horses.

They will be ready, eager to gallop,
I will not have to guide them.
They know the way.
They know the smell of salt.

Then,
Clenching their manes,
Hungering for the tides,
I will be riding again.

I have come the way they said was
Impossible.

From the meadows, into the forest,
Down the ravine.
There, where the path ends,
Is a sea of stones,

Enormous boulders, unnavigable whirlpools —
I crossed them.
Then, there is the world of ice —
The prisms, the down slides, the cataracts.

After I had come through,
I rested
Before embarking for the island of fire.
Later, singed, I paused again

Before making the climb
To this precipitous pinnacle of dust.
Naturally, the view is clouded.
It is easier to see behind than beyond.

But my feet are slipping,
A final journey is inevitable,
And it promises to be no easier
Than the way I have come.

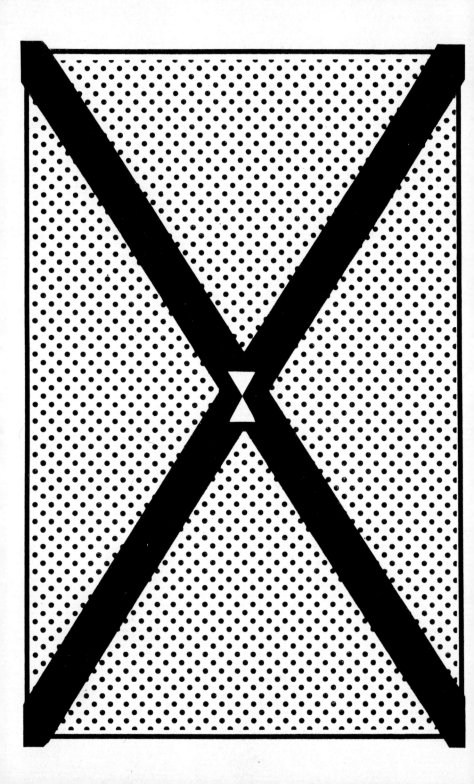